'I found this book easy to read. I think that
using plasticine and big letters to learn
spellings can help more than writing on a

...... word.

— Aaron, age 14

'I like how the book tells you how to do the
games. I don't like to learn spellings normally,
sitting down and writing them over and
over again. I like to have more fun when I'm
learning.'

— Cameron, dyslexic child, age 11

'We all have different styles of learning
and learn at different rates. Being dyslexic
emphasizes this. Alais has tutored our son
George for the last 18 months and used
these methods successfully to capture his
great imagination. He is now learning with
confidence and improving as a result. Alais
understands what being dyslexic means and
is able to adapt teaching techniques to get
proven results.'

— Neal and Victoria,
parents to George, age 10

by the same author

The Self-Help Guide for Teens with Dyslexia
Useful Stuff You May Not Learn at School
Alais Winton
ISBN 978 1 84905 649 6
eISBN 978 1 78450 144 0

of related interest

The Illustrated Guide to Dyslexia
and Its Amazing People
Kate Power & Kathy Iwanczak Forsyth
Foreword by Richard Rogers
ISBN 978 1 78592 330 2
eISBN 978 1 78450 647 6

Can I tell you about Dyslexia?
A guide for friends, family and professionals
Alan M. Hultquist
Illustrated by Bill Tulp
ISBN 978 1 84905 952 7
eISBN 978 0 85700 810 7
Part of the Can I tell you about...? *series*

Dyslexia is My Superpower (Most of the Time)
Margaret Rooke
Forewords by Professor Catherine L. Drennan and Loyle Carner
ISBN 978 1 78592 299 2
eISBN 978 1 78450 606 3

Creative, Successful, Dyslexic
23 High Achievers Share Their Stories
Margaret Rooke
Foreword by Mollie King
ISBN 978 1 84905 653 3 (Hardback)
ISBN 978 1 78592 060 8 (Paperback)
eISBN 978 1 78450 163 1

I Don't Like Reading
Lisabeth Emlyn Clark
ISBN 978 1 78592 354 8
eISBN 978 1 78450 693 3

Fun Games and Activities for Children with Dyslexia

How to Learn Smarter with a Dyslexic Brain

Alais Winton

Illustrated by Joe Salerno

Jessica Kingsley *Publishers*
London and Philadelphia

First published in 2018
by Jessica Kingsley Publishers
73 Collier Street
London N1 9BE, UK
and
400 Market Street, Suite 400
Philadelphia, PA 19106, USA

www.jkp.com

Copyright © Alais Winton 2018
Illustrations copyright © Joe Salerno 2018

Library of Congress Cataloging in Publication Data
A CIP catalog record for this book is available
from the Library of Congress

British Library Cataloguing in Publication Data
A CIP catalogue record for this book is available from the British Library

ISBN 978 1 78592 292 3
eISBN 978 1 78450 596 7

Printed and bound in Great Britain

MIX
Paper from
responsible sources
FSC
www.fsc.org   FSC® C013056

For anyone who has ever felt like giving up on learning – I believe in you.

For all those who have helped me to not give up on my goals, by believing in me.

Acknowledgements

Thank you to Joe Salerno for fantastic
illustrations, understanding my
ideas and giving them life.

Many thanks to Harriet Hughes for your
amazing contributions to the book.

Thanks also to Jenna for trying new
ways of learning, and Rebecca for
your support and feedback.

Many thanks to George Morgan, Aaron
Loosmore, Oliver Reed and Rio Massebo
for the wonderful contributions and
inspiration that you have given me.

This book would not have happened without
input from all those named above.

Thanks to all of your families for continued
support for the work and ideas in this book.

Thank you to Sian Jenkins for
feedback on Chapter 9, and to
Cameron for the best quote ever.

Special thanks to Gordon for proofing my work and living with a dyslexic writer.

Many thanks to Rachel Menzies for suggesting a second book.

Thanks also to Emily Badger and all at Jessica Kingsley Publishers, for all their hard work and patient answering of my questions.

Thank you to Alaric for words of wisdom and always believing that I would write another book.

Thanks to Alex for being my friend and for her continued promotion and support of the tuition work.

Thanks to Hannah, for all the good times, for being there for me in the bad times and for always keeping the faith.

Thank you to any of my current or past clients not already mentioned by name.

Finally, thanks to everyone else who has helped and supported me in the writing of this book.

Contents

CHAPTER 1

A Very Special Letter

My name is Alais (pronounced 'Alice') and I am dyslexic.

Being dyslexic can mean different things to different people, but it usually means that spelling and reading can be difficult.

The good thing about being dyslexic is that it can mean that you are very creative and can think in pictures instead of words.

Some time ago I was sent a very special letter. It was written by Hannah, who was ten when she wrote the letter.

I had spoken to Hannah's mum on the phone and she told me that Hannah was finding spelling tests and reading in school hard.

Hannah wanted to write me a letter to tell me what being dyslexic was like for her. This is what she wrote:

Dear Alais Winton,

I find Dyslexia as a good thing but then also a bad thing.

One good thing is I get a lot of support in my class.

My mum says that people who are dyslexic succeed and I believe her.

My teacher tries to teach me but in writing and reading I sometimes don't get it.

One bad thing is in class I feel like I'm not as good as other people.

Some teachers just make me do easy work.

Sometimes I have to move away from my friends, which makes me feel sad as I have no support from the other children on that table.

I love Drama and Art and History.

In school I find spelling hard and usually get four out of fifteen, maybe ten out of fifteen, which is not a lot according to my teacher.

Hopefully you can help me as I feel left out, and not as good as other people.

I was really moved by Hannah's letter. She did make some spelling mistakes (which I have corrected), but I was able to understand everything she was saying in this letter.

When I was in school I remember feeling the same as Hannah: sometimes I just didn't get it and I couldn't understand why.

I didn't find out that I was dyslexic until I was eighteen and, when I did, I wasn't sure at first what it meant.

I think Hannah was really brave and honest in her letter, and it made me very sad to hear that she didn't feel as good as other people.

I have been a teacher for a long time (and a learner, too) and I really believe that learning should be fun and make you feel good about yourself by finding out what you are good at.

I did some work with Hannah. When I met her I realised that, even though she found spelling and reading harder than people who were not dyslexic, she was very bright.

She thinks about things very deeply, and has at times asked me questions that adults may not have thought of.

People think in different ways because we don't all have the same kind of brain.

This means that people also learn in different ways.

Most subjects in school (apart from Art and Drama) have a teacher standing at the front of the class explaining what is on the board, and the children write notes.

For many people, especially those who are dyslexic, this method does not work very well.

If your English and Maths lessons are not often like this, you probably have a super smart teacher who might also be a bit of a rebel – lucky you!

But if sitting and writing notes sounds like the classes at your school, and it doesn't work well for you, take the following quiz to find out what is your best learning style.

You may get a high score in more than one area; this will just mean that you can 'mix and match' and choose which method you want to use.

Learning styles statements: Is it true for you?

Read these statements and decide whether they are true for you, answering 'yes', 'maybe' or 'no'. Score one point for 'yes', half a point for 'maybe' and zero points for 'no'. Add up the totals for each style and see which method works best for you.

Visual-Spatial (picture thinker) – best games and activities found in Chapters 2 and 3

◯ You think in images or pictures and not in words.

◯ You often find yourself doodling when you are making notes.

◯ You find it easier to understand something if there is a diagram, picture or video.

◯ You prefer games which use visual skills, for example 'Pictionary', 'pairs' or a games console.

◯ You can imagine how things would look from different points of view.

Physical (movement thinker) – best games and activities found in Chapters 2 and 4

○ You prefer PE and practical lessons.

○ You like to think about things whilst doing something physical, such as walking or running.

○ You find it difficult to sit still in class and other people have described you as a 'fidget'.

○ You take part in a sport or exercise outside of school time.

○ If you are learning something new, you prefer to do this in an active 'hands on' way, rather than read a book or follow written or verbal instructions.

**Musical (music thinker) –
best games and activities
found in Chapter 5**

○ You listen to music on your
MP3 player or phone whenever
you can.

○ You wouldn't want to think about
a world without music.

○ You play an instrument or sing.

○ You often find yourself thinking
of music from TV programmes
or adverts.

○ When you listen to music you find
yourself tapping out the beat.

Interpersonal (people person)
– best games and activities
found in Chapter 6

◯ You like to work with other people as part of a team.

◯ Other people come to you to ask for advice.

◯ You are good at talking to people and sorting out any arguments.

◯ You are sociable and would rather be out with friends than home alone.

◯ You prefer to talk about any problems with other people rather than trying to deal with them by yourself.

(Adapted from Gardener 2006)

Make a note of which style your highest score was in.

You could try activities and games from all the following chapters but the one about your strongest learning style will usually work best for you. So, why not start with that chapter first and then check out the rest. You may find that you get a high score in more than one learning style – this just means that you can mix and match activities from different chapters.

CHAPTER 2

Make It!

I learn best through what I can see and what I do

This chapter will explain a different way to learn how to spell words.

▶ Spelling sculptures

This activity will be helpful to anyone who scored high in the learning styles quiz in visual-spatial learning (picture thinker) or physical learning (movement thinker), since the colour and image will suit a visual brain and the 'hands on' bit of the task will suit a physical brain.

What to do

Make a list of words which have been spelt incorrectly. This could be:

- Words misspelt for a spelling test you have already done

- Words in written work corrected by a teacher

- Words from a mind map or homework that a parent has corrected

- Words you have been told to learn how to spell for a test or exam.

Only work on six or seven words at a time. Difficult words to spell could include **friend** and **guitar** as they are spelt differently to how they sound.

Make sure you have the correct spelling to hand or ask someone to help you.

Lay out the correct spelling using letters from a bathtime alphabet set as a guide.

Make each letter using plasticine. Use a different colour for each letter and make sure each letter can stand up.

Spend some time looking at your plasticine sculpture (anything between 30 seconds and 3 minutes). Try to think of this as a piece of artwork and not a word.

Close your eyes and try to picture your sculpture in your mind. If you are unsure, look again and then close your eyes again.

With your eyes closed, say what colour the first and last letters are, and then, still with your eyes closed, speak each letter out loud in the correct order.

It is useful if a parent or friend can tell you if you are getting it right, but it is possible to check for yourself when you open your eyes again.

You could also ask someone to test you again a few days later to make sure it really has 'stuck' in your mind.

CHAPTER 3

Picture It!

> I learn best through what I can see

Spelling longer words

The plasticine method explained in Chapter 2 is useful for words of seven letters or less, but can take a lot of time for longer words.

If you learn very well through pictures and images, this could be a good way to remember how to spell longer words.

A longer word that I worked on with a young person, not long ago, was **competition**.

If you say the word out loud you will notice that it isn't spelt exactly the same way that it sounds, so it is a common word to make mistakes with.

First of all we used a very well-known idea of making up a sentence with each word in the sentence starting with the first letter matching each of the letters in the word.

So, for the word **competition**, the sentence was:

Cats **O**nly **m**eet **p**andas **e**very **t**uesday **i**f **t**hey **i**ce-skate **O**n **n**eptune.

This is a long sentence to remember so we took it one step further and drew a picture to match the sentence.

The picture included a panda ice-skating on Neptune and cats looking at a newspaper with Tuesday written on it.

You don't have to be fantastic at art to do this; as long as you know what you have drawn, your picture will act as a good reminder.

For some words you might not need to do the whole word but just key letters.

For example, for the word **address** it is important to remember the two **d**s and two **s**s, so you might say: 'Write an address to **d**eliver **d**ocument, **S**eeking **S**omeone', and then draw a picture to go with it.

For the word **succeed** it is important to remember the two **c**s and two **e**s, so you could say: 'You need to be **C**reative and have **C**ommitment, **e**nergy and **e**nthusiasm to succeed.'

You could then draw a picture of someone showing they are being creative, energetic, committed and enthusiastic: maybe someone painting a wall and not giving up even if parts of it are hard to reach.

You may already know parts of the word and could just focus on the tricky bit.

So, in the word **knowledgeable** you could use the following sentence:

I **know l**ions **e**at **d**onkeys, and **g**iraffes **e**scape because they are **able** to.

Try to figure out what the hard bits of the word are. It will usually be patterns in words that you haven't seen before and parts of the word which are spelt differently to how they sound.

▶ Word jigsaw

For this activity you could use a list of words given to you by your school for a spelling test, or you could choose your own words.

You can make this game harder by choosing words that all end with the same letters.

For example, words which end with **ent**:

- **sent**   - **consent**

- **tent**   - **prevent**

- **rent**

Once you have chosen your list of words, write them on cardboard – the kind that is sold in packs for craft work.

Make sure you leave plenty of space between letters and write the words as large as you can.

Cut out each word. Then cut the words up into sections of two or three letters together.

You can make these cuts as a curve, an S shape or cut them on a diagonal; as long as the letters will fit back together you can be as creative as you like.

Mix up all the pieces you have cut up. You could do this by turning them upside down and then moving them around on a table.

Then look at the pieces and try to fit the words back together like a jigsaw.

If you like to draw, you could write all of your words in a shape (a star, for example) and then, when you put your jigsaw together, it will make your shape again.

▶ Homophone pairs game

A homophone is the name for a word which sounds the same as another word, but is spelt differently and has different meanings. For example, 'I'm lost, **where** should I go?' and 'What can I **wear** to the party tonight?'

If you spell words like they sound, as most dyslexics do, these sorts of words can be very tricky, so it is worth learning some that are used a lot.

To make your pairs

Cut out eight squares from two pieces of card, so that you have 16 squares in total.

Next, write a homophone word in eight of the squares. You can use the following example words or think of your own:

- sail
- where

- sale
- wear

- pear
- knot

- pair
- not

On the rest of the cards, draw a picture which shows the meaning of the word.

For example, for the word **sail**, you could draw a boat with sails, and for **sale** you could draw something with a price tag to show that it is for sale.

For **pear** you could draw the fruit, and for **pair** you could draw a pair of shoes or socks.

For **knot** you could draw a rope tied in a knot, and for **not** you could draw something you're not supposed to do and put a line through it to show that it is not allowed.

Once you have made all the cards, mix them up and put them face down on the floor or on a table.

Then turn over two cards at a time. If they match the right word with the picture that shows what the word means you have won a pair and can keep both cards.

If the cards do not match, turn them face down in the same place and then either try again (if it is just you playing) or the next player has a turn.

If you do win a pair then you get another go before the next player takes their turn.

At the end of the game each player counts the number of pairs they have, to see who has won.

CHAPTER 4

Shake It!

I learn best through movement

This chapter is for a learner who learns very well through movement.

This can be really difficult in school. Apart from subjects like PE and Drama, most classes will involve quite a lot of sitting still and writing.

Learning to spell words through movement is quite easy and can be great fun.

You could do this alone or with a friend or parent.

Make sure you start with the right spelling of the word you want to learn.

This could include words you have been given from school to learn as homework or something you have asked someone to look up for you.

Once you can see the correct spelling of the word, use a different part of your body to make each letter.

For example, for the word **ancient** you could use your shoulder for the letter **a**, your knee for the letter **n**, your elbow for the letter **c**, and so on, until you get to the end of the word.

Practise your body spelling as many times as you like and ask someone to test you on the same word the next day.

For the test, you could use a paintbrush to invisibly paint the word in the air and speak each letter as you 'paint' it.

Capital letter dance-off

If you are dyslexic, the use of capital letters can be tricky.

Some of the young people I work with use capital letters in sentences when they are not needed, some miss out capital letters when they should be used, and some people do both of these things.

There are clear rules about when a capital letter is needed.

If you learn best through movement, make up a dance move which stands for each rule.

When to use capital letters

- At the start of a sentence

- At the start of speech

- The title of a book, or chapter heading

- Direct reference to yourself: **I**

- Place names, including planets (e.g. **Venus**)

- People's names

- Days of the week, months of the year, special holidays (e.g. **Christmas** and **Easter**)

- Brand names (e.g. **Pixar**)

- Titles (e.g. **Ms**, **Mr**, **Lord**, **Lady**)

- Abbreviation (e.g. **NASA**, which stands for **N**ational **A**eronautics **S**pace **A**dministration).

Your dance move could be something which links to the rule.

For example, opening doors to suggest the start of a sentence, or using your hands to make speech marks (bunny ears) for the start of speech.

My [open door] sister said, 'Don't [bunny ears] play with that, it's mine.'

Or you could just use your own crazy dance moves. Get creative!

Once you have come up with a set of moves, teach it to a partner. This could be a friend or family member.

Then take it in turns to do each move. The person not doing the move must say what the reason is for that movement.

If you want to get competitive, you could score a point for every correct answer.

When you have done this a few times, ask someone to read something out loud and do the movement for each capital letter.

Here are some examples you could read out:

Last week **I** went to **L**ondon to see the **Q**ueen, but she wasn't at home.

When I got back my cat said, '**D**id you see the **Q**ueen?'

I said, '**S**he wasn't there, but **I** got you some **W**hiskas to cheer you up.'

Games and **A**ctivities for **C**hildren with **D**yslexia (a title).

Miss **T**homas misses her **T**etley tea.

If you meet the **Q**ueen you call her **M**a'am; if you write to her you call her **Y**our **M**ajesty.

A judge is **Y**our **H**onour, and a duke is **Y**our **G**race. **A** member of parliament is known as an **MP** and a doctor is a **GP** (general practitioner).

Some words can be a real challenge, as sometimes they need a capital letter and sometimes they don't.

For example, in the sentence 'She was a pretty **l**ady', you don't need a capital letter for lady as this could be about any woman.

However, in the sentence 'It was kind of **L**ady Felicia to invite us', you would need to use a capital letter for the word Lady as it is a title for a specific person.

In the same way if you wrote 'King Richard's **d**eath was tragic', the word death does not need a capital letter.

However, if it is a character name, for example, 'Scrooge was visited by **D**eath', it does need a capital letter.

You can test yourself in a Yes/No game using the table on the next page (or make up your own words).

GODS	AIRPORT	LADY	PLANETS
GOD	MR BEN	OCTOBER	PE
CHRISTMAS	NEPTUNE	CASTLES	DEATH
MYSELF	JELLY	NEWCASTLE	TOMORROW
I	QUEEN	STARBURST	PEOPLE

▶ Treasure hunts

Treasure hunts can be great fun and can easily be done indoors.

You could hunt for Scrabble tiles or letter cards to form the correct spelling for words. Or you could find the meanings to match word cards, for example:

- **typhoon** (word card)

- a hurricane or bad storm (meaning card).

Ask a parent or friend to hide the letter or meaning cards around the room. Then get that person to tell you the word (to check the spelling of the word) or pick word cards at random (to practise matching word meanings).

Next, search the room for either the letters to create the correct spelling or for the right meaning for the word chosen.

The treasure could be anything (such as a reward sticker, bookmark, party prize, etc.).

You could ask someone to tell you how many answers you need to find in order to win your 'treasure'.

▶ Times tables

In the classroom, multiplications (times tables) are usually taught by rote.

This means that the teacher says them out loud and the class repeat them several times.

This way of learning does not work for everyone, and you may find that your times tables just don't sink in.

You may also find that you can do some sets of multiplication (e.g. 2s, 5s and 10s) but find other sets (e.g. 7s) more of a challenge.

For the following activity you will need all the times tables questions and answers.

If possible, the tables should be colourful with large writing so that it is easy to find each set of times tables.

You could use a times tables board (see Resources) instead.

Mine is like a giant wooden jigsaw with a different colour for each set (e.g. 7s are purple).

The question is on the front of each tile (e.g. 6 × 7) and the answer is printed on the back of the tile (e.g. 42).

Once you have the answers, choose
a number from 1 to 10 that you would
like to work on, then you can begin
the activity.

Find a wall on which you can see your
shadow. Try putting on a lamp behind
you if this helps.

Next, say the question out loud
(e.g. 1 × 7) and then, using your hand
and arm, make the shadow of the
answer (e.g. 7) on the wall.

Work through the whole set in
sequence using the tables to help with
answers that you are unsure of.

Then, using your feet (your left for
tens and your right for numbers 1 to 9),
repeat the activity by drawing the
answers on the floor.

Use the book or board to test yourself.

Make sure you try using a different order (e.g. 5 × 7, then 3 × 7, etc.) to check that it is in your memory and you aren't just adding on (7) each time.

Mathematical problems

Here is an example of a basic maths problem:

> **Jane has 10 penguins. She gives 3 to Simon, who gives her 2 back.**
>
> **Peter gives Jane 6 penguins, 2 ducks and 4 hats.**
>
> **Jill borrows 1 of the hats and takes 9 penguins for her zoo.**
>
> **How many penguins and how many hats does Jane have left?**

You have probably come across similar problems in your maths class at school.

I used to find this sort of thing very confusing.

I could never get the order right in my head, or keep track of who had what, or who was where, at any point in the puzzle.

Physical props can be really useful in working through something like this.

For example, for the problem above you will need four bits of LEGO® or Cluedo playing pieces, each standing in for the people in the problem (e.g. Jane could be the yellow piece).

Next, you will need the other items in the problem.

So, in this case, the items would be penguins, ducks and hats.

It is possible to buy penguin erasers, plastic ducks and to make small hats easily out of plasticine.

To make a small hat using plasticine, roll a small very short sausage shape and flatten each end by gently pressing it onto a table.

Then make a small flat roundish shape for the brim and attach the two pieces together.

I just did this and it was quick and fun!

Once you have all your 'people' and items on the table, work through each line of the problem moving things and animals as directed.

Using the following problem:

Jane has 10 penguins. She gives 3 to Simon, who gives her 2 back.

Place 10 penguins next to Jane (yellow Cluedo piece), then move 3 over to Simon (purple), then move 2 back to Jane. You will see that Jane now has 9 penguins.

Peter gives Jane 6 penguins, 2 ducks and 4 hats.

Peter (blue) moves 6 penguins, 2 ducks and 4 hats to Jane. You will see that Jane now has 15 penguins, 2 ducks and 4 hats.

Jill borrows 1 of the hats and takes 9 penguins for her zoo.

Move 1 hat and 9 penguins from Jane to Jill (green). You will see that Jane now has 6 penguins, 2 ducks and 3 hats.

You can ignore the number of ducks as the question does not ask about them.

So the answer is:

Jane has 6 penguins and 3 hats.

CHAPTER 5

Hear It, Sing It, Beat It!

I learn best through music

▶ Tap it out!

If music is your thing, it can really help with learning, especially memory. You probably know all the words to your favourite songs without even trying to learn them.

This is partly due to repetition (you will have listened to the song more than once), but also because the tune (the music) helps you to remember.

Alex is very musical; he has guitar lessons two or three times a week. He also scored very high in the 'learning though music' section of the learner quiz.

Like many people, Alex finds it difficult to remember long sequences of numbers (lots of numbers in a particular order).

The following activity really helped.

If you also learn well through music, you might like to try it.

What you will need

- A metronome (or electronic beat counter)

- A craft stick, lollipop stick, paint brush or similar

- A list of numbers to be remembered in order

- Pen and paper.

How to do the activity

Start the metronome on a slow count and for a beat of four counts per bar.

Have the list of numbers in front of you.

Use the craft stick to tap out each number in time with the beats of the metronome.

For example, if the first number is two, tap two beats and then wait for the next two beats for the start of the next bar. Counting out loud as you tap is also useful.

If the number is bigger than four you will need to carry on into the next bar.

So the number seven would mean tapping all four beats in the first bar and then carrying on for three beats of the next bar.

Once you have counted and tapped up to seven, leave the last beat not tapped or counted before starting the next number at the start of the next bar.

Repeat the whole set of numbers like this at least three times. Then, without looking at your list, write down all the numbers in the right order.

You could tap out each number before writing it down if this helps.

▶ Jingle bones

The next activity is about learning the names for bones in the body, but you could use the same method for any lists you need to remember, from spelling test words to dates and facts for history.

I worked with Jess who wanted to learn the names of the main bones of the human skeleton, from the skull (head) to the phalanges (toes).

Although Jess works well with pictures and a diagram was useful, one of her main strengths in learning is music.

I asked Jess what her favourite Christmas song was and she said it was 'Jingle Bells'.

You could choose any song you want but, if you are doing this activity with a family member, Christmas songs will be known by people of different ages; otherwise, Dad or Grandma might not know how your favourite song goes.

Once you have decided what you would like to learn, and have the information in front of you, just change the words of the song to what you want to remember.

You might have to add in words to fit the music, for example 'and then', 'next' or 'leading to'.

If you want to repeat the same words in the chorus each time this will also help, so you might want to put some of the harder stuff to remember in the chorus as you will sing it more than once each time you sing the song.

You could try this to the tune of 'Jingle Bells':

Your bones help you to stand up,

Your joints help you to move,

Your skull protects your brain,

And your ribs protect your heart.

(Chorus)

Calcium, keeps them strong

So, look after your bones,

Short or flat or long, your

Body needs 'em as it grows, OH!

(Repeat chorus)

Before Jess had her test she hummed Jingle Bells to herself and then remembered the names of the bones.

You can sing it as many times as you want, until you feel like you know whatever it is that you wanted to remember.

The joy of singing it

Most people learn the alphabet song when they are very young.

If you haven't learnt this at school, ask an adult to teach you.

I still use the alphabet song when I want to look something up in a dictionary or when I need to put words in alphabetical order.

You'll probably be asked to do this in secondary school (11 plus), if not before.

When you are at home you could also have a go at singing a page in a book instead of reading it.

If you love music you will enjoy it more, but it could also help you to read linking words correctly as you will take more time and so your brain is less likely to guess smaller words and fill in the gaps.

For example, **from** can be mistaken for **form** or **for**, **then** or **them** can be mistaken for **than**, and so on.

These words can be even trickier if you are dyslexic, as they are words which don't have an image which naturally goes with them, unlike words such as **horse**, **church** or **tree** which can all be linked to picture memory.

If you know that you find it difficult getting these words right when you read, you could also try reading in slow motion.

Slow your voice down as much as you can – it can be very funny!

You could try this with just a paragraph (if you do a whole book like this it could take a very long time!).

▶ An English rap

For English lessons you will need to know certain words and what they mean.

For example, a verb is a doing word: a word for some kind of action or activity, like drawing.

I worked with a boy (who was 11 at the time) who helped me to come up with the following rap to help remember the different words and examples of their meanings:

You might be hot or you might be cold, these are antonyms, so I'm told.

The antonym of up, is always down.

Now let's talk about a noun: a word to name things, people and places, to help me put names to faces.

Pronouns are used when you used a noun before. So: it, he, she, his – you know the score.

I bought a <u>pair</u> of shoes, and then I ate a <u>pear</u>. These are homophones, so when spelling take care.

If you want a contraction, <u>don't</u> tell me what to do. <u>It's</u> now one word, when it used to be two.

Compound words are like this as well, but no need for the apostrophe – you can probably tell – <u>football</u> yeah!

If you want to do something, you're gonna need a verb, like climbing or swimming, or so I've heard.

CHAPTER 6

Say It, Play It!

> I learn through talking and teamwork

If you like drama and working with others to solve problems, then this chapter is for you.

I have always loved drama, and acting things out can be a really good way to remember things.

Some letters behave in a set way and always sound the same (like the letter **V**), and others can change their sound depending on the word (like the letter **C**).

Here are a couple of plays you could act out with a friend, to help you remember how **V** and **C** behave in words.

Play 1 – The Story of V

E: Hey V, how are you?

V: Not good.

E: Why, what's wrong?

V: Some of the other letters make fun of me at Letter School.

E: Who's making fun of you?

V: The consonants mostly. Especially K. He says that I'm only half a W.

E: I will stick up for you, don't worry.

V: It's not just the other letters I'm afraid of.

E: What else are you scared of?

V: Spiders, loud noises, beetroot. But mostly the big white spaces on a page. And punctuation, commas, full stops. That sort of thing.

E: What's scary about white spaces?

V: I don't ever want to be on the end of a word. What if I get sucked into the space, the void?

E: I'll protect you. I will also talk to the other vowels. They really like you. We will protect you as much as we can from consonants and we will always follow you at the end of a word, so you are never next to the white space on your own.

V: Thanks E, you're my best friend!

Play 2 – The Changing Face of C

H: What's up, C? How was your day?

C: Not bad. I've been hanging out with R today – we made **crab** and **creatures**, **crawling** on the ground; it was fun. Where's L?

H: She's getting ready for this fancy dress party. Are you going?

C: Yes, definitely! I love fancy dress!

H: What are you going as?

C: I don't know. Who's going to be there?

H: Hmm...let me think. Well, it's E's party, so he will be there and I think I and Y are going. You know all of them don't you?

C: Yeah, they're a great crowd. But if they're all going to be there, I will go as the letter S.

H: Why are you going as the letter S?

C: Because then we can make words like: **ceiling**, **cycle** and **circle** and those words are great. You need **circle** just to be able to turn all the way around.

H: Won't S mind if you turn up as her?

C: No, not if I'm hanging out with I, Y and E. If she comes over she'll just hang out in a different bit of the word or make plurals all night. She loves doing that.

H: Okay. Well, have a good time and try not to fall over; everyone thought that you were a U last time that happened!

C: Ha, ha, see you later.

▶ Shh silent letters game

Silent letters in words can be really hard for anyone who has dyslexia, because that person will often spell things how they sound. So if there is a letter that cannot be heard, it will probably get missed out.

Here are some examples with the silent letter in bold print:

- **G**nome
- **K**night
- We**d**nesday
- Dou**b**t
- Desi**g**n
- R**h**ythm

- Autum**n**
- Recei**p**t
- **W**rap
- Ans**w**er
- Sof**t**en
- S**w**ord

You can see from these examples that the silent letter can be at the start of the word, in the middle or at the end of the word.

The best way to deal with this challenge is to learn the most common ones.

You could try the following game to help you.

Make some cards with silent letter words. Here are some examples:

Shh! Don't say the B in Doubt.	Shh! Don't say the G in Gnome.	Shh! Don't say the W in Answer.	Shh! Don't say the K in Knight.

You could use the examples above, or from a list from school or get a parent to choose some.

You will also need some cards with silent letters on them. Here are some examples:

B	G	W	K

Two players can act out silent letter cards.

- The first player chooses a word card and keeps it hidden from the second player.

- The first player then reads just the word on the card out loud; for example, 'thumb'.

- The second player then chooses a letter card and uses it as a prompt to ask, for example, 'Does your word have a silent **b**?'

- If the answer is 'no', the second player picks another letter card and tries again.

- If the answer is 'yes', the first player reads all of the word card out loud, for example, 'Shh! Don't say the **b** in thum**b**.'

- When the first player can give their 'Shh!' response, players can then swap roles and repeat with a different word card.

- Carry on until all the word cards have been used.

If you want to play this with more players, just make sure that you swap roles so that every player gets a chance to guess the silent letter.

▶ Word of the week

This is something the whole family can take part in.

Choose one member of your family to be the 'judge'.

Everyone, apart from the judge, finds a word which is new to them. This could be something you read, see at school or hear on television.

Find out the meaning of the word and check the spelling, then write the word and a short meaning on a piece of paper. Fold it carefully and put it in a jar.

At the end of the week the judge opens the jar and looks at the words and reads them out.

They then choose the one that they like the most. The person who wrote that word is the winner and could get a star sticker.

The next week a different member of the family can be the judge while the activity is played out again.

Change judges each week until everyone has had a turn at being the judge.

This can be a fun way to talk about and learn new words.

▶ Police line up

This is a good game to help with spelling.

You will need word cards: one with the correct spelling, and two or three with the wrong spelling of the same word. For example:

Family	Famlie	Famely

or

Tuna	Tooner	Chuna

Draw faces, hats, beards, etc. on the words to make them look like people.

Lay each of the words out in a police line up, and then find the one which is the right spelling.

You could arrest the other words for not being spelt correctly, or you could arrest the one that is right. It's up to you.

You could play this on your own, or with your friends and family.

▶ Happy families

This is based on a card game that you may have heard of, called 'Happy Families'.

The aim of the game is very simple: you are trying to collect a whole family of each set.

In this version, instead of using jobs (e.g. Mrs Bun the Baker), you are using words.

Some cards have one letter (e.g. V or W) or two letters together (e.g. SN or GR).

You will need to start by making your own letter cards, four for each member of the letter/letter's family, as shown on the next page:

Mrs	Miss	Mr	Master
V	V	V	V
Mrs	Miss	Mr	Master
SN	SN	SN	SN

When you have all the different letters, cut them out and then shuffle them and deal an equal number of cards to each player.

It is possible to play this with two people, but you will know which cards the other person has, so it is better played with three or more players.

When it is your turn you must first of all name the person you want to ask.

Once you have done that, if you wanted a member of the V family, you could ask that player: 'Do you have

Mrs V, as in...' and think of a word beginning with the letter V (e.g. violin).

If you wanted a member of the SN family you would need to think of a word starting with those two letters.

For example, 'Do you have Mr SN as in...(snail, for example)?' or 'Do you have Miss SN as in...(snooze, perhaps)?'

If the answer to your question is yes, then you are given the card you asked for, and you take another turn.

If the person you asked does not have that card, then they say 'No, sorry, she's/he's not at home.'

It then becomes the turn of the person you asked.

When you have collected a family (all four cards in a set), put them face down beside you.

At the end of the game each player counts the number of families that they have and the player with the most wins.

You could adapt this version by giving extra points for longer words (more than four letters) or for words which are less well-known.

CHAPTER 7

Handwriting

Making Your Mark

Two of the young people I have been working with told me that they wanted to improve their handwriting.

I wanted to try something different with them.

When learning to write letters, most people will copy letters many times to perfect the shape, so this method had probably already been tried and had not made a big difference.

This also does not take into account any difficulty that someone might have with writing in a straight line (even on lined paper).

This is something I still find challenging at times.

I asked them to try the following activities, which you could also try.

▶ Handwriting improvement exercises

(Ideas featured in: Practice Exercises for Adults, Teens and Older Kids to Improve Handwriting at **http:// feltmagnet.com, author: Natasha)**

Hand skills

- Using the hand that you write with, crumple up a piece of paper.

- Using a soft ball, roll the ball around on a hard surface, using the hand that you write with. Roll the ball up to your elbow and back and roll it around with your hand for a second time, moving it to the outer edge of your fingers this time.

- Using the hand that you write with, break plasticine into 3 small pieces. Then use your thumb, the finger next to it and your middle finger to create a pincer/triangle shape. When that position has been formed, use your thumb and fingers to roll the plasticine into a ball.

Practice tasks

You will need lined paper (preferably wide-lined).

- Within the lines, draw a series of parallel vertical lines. Try to make them straight and the same length.

- Within the lines, draw a series of horizontal lines. Try to make them straight and the same length. Try to fit three lines between each pair of lines on the page.

- Draw clouds inside the lines to practise the curves of some letters.

- Repeat as often as possible and monitor improvement in your handwriting.

I also suggested:

- using a large paint brush to draw straight lines in the air.

- using the same brush to draw out a letter that they wanted to improve whilst closing their eyes and thinking of a perfect image of that letter.

Case studies

David

I have been working with David for about a year. David's mum said that she would like David's writing to be easier to read.

I had also noticed in written work which David had done with me that some letters and words could be clearer.

When I talked to David about his handwriting he told me that he would like some letters, especially **b**s, **d**s and **u**s, to be clearer.

David used the practice tasks explained above (lines and clouds). He also used my suggestion of imagining a perfect letter in his head and then drawing it in the air with a paint brush.

David carried out these exercises three times a day, every day, for two weeks.

After two weeks of practice, David's mum and I both saw a big improvement in his handwriting.

David's letters looked much clearer, neater, straighter and easier to read.

David is still doing the exercises often and plans to keep doing them to carry on making his writing clearer and straighter.

David's mum said that it would be a good idea to do the lines practice in short bursts, as it is repetitive and so could become boring.

David said he had found the exercises useful and he would recommend them to friends, as it could help improve their handwriting.

Morgan

Morgan's parents told me that they would like us to do some work on his handwriting in one of our review sessions.

In the reviews we talk about progress and future goals.

Morgan did not think that he needed to make any individual letters clearer, but he did want his sentences to be on a straight line and his writing to be easier to read.

Morgan did the handwriting improvement exercises once a week for six weeks.

Morgan was nine at the time of these exercises and is very creative so, instead of using the patterns of lines and clouds on lined paper, he used them to draw images on plain paper instead.

His images included a person on a boat, an aeroplane and robots.

The image he created, using the line and cloud patterns to draw robots, has been used as this chapter's picture.

After about three weeks of doing these exercises there was a visible improvement in Morgan's handwriting and this improvement was noticed by his teachers at school.

Morgan says he will carry on with the exercises and would definitely recommend them to a friend.

Morgan's handwriting was also helped by using the special handwriting-friendly pen (see Resources). He gave the pen a five-star rating.

CHAPTER 8

Let Not Giving Up
Be Your Thing

A few weeks ago I met someone called Cuba (aged 11).

His stepmother had asked me to run a one-off session for him and his sister.

Cuba is the reason I wanted to write this chapter.

Cuba is a bright, active and cool young person.

However, the reading and writing methods used in school, especially for English lessons, do not appeal to the way his brain learns best.

Cuba learns best through both pictures and movement, but is probably slightly more drawn to movement.

Cuba did really well in our session together and was able to spell words worked on through movement, quickly and correctly.

He was also able to repeat the activity with different words later that day.

However, during the session, we were searching for a sticker letter which was proving tricky to find. When his stepmother told him not to give up, he said, 'But that's what I do. Giving up is my thing.'

It made me very sad to think that the things Cuba has experienced in learning have made him feel this way at the age of 11.

When I was young it took me a lot longer to learn things than my sibling or my friends.

I'm sure that because of this there were times when I felt like giving up. But I never did.

Some people are able to learn things very quickly for a test or exam but then forget most or all of it after the test – I have seen this in teaching.

If it takes you longer to learn something, you are more likely to understand it better and remember it for longer.

When I think of people I come into contact with who have different jobs – hairdresser, doctor, mechanic, and so on – I want that person to really know their stuff and understand it well, even if it took them longer to learn it in the first place.

I often talk to the young people I work with about the idea of climbing a very tall mountain.

I ask them to think about what it would be like if I said we were going to climb Mount Everest tomorrow, with no training, preparation or practice.

They all agree it would be too hard –
we couldn't do it!

Then we talk about what it would
be like if we had a year to prepare,
did lots of exercise and started
by practising on smaller hills and
mountains.

This would take hard work and
determination, but climbing the
mountain would then be possible.

If you think of Mount Everest as a big
test or exam, the same idea applies;
smaller steps beforehand will make it
easier to conquer.

▶ Count to 10

This is a game you could play to test how determined you are.

Everyone playing (the more players the better) sits in a circle.

Then, as a group, you count to ten. This may sound easy but the rules make it harder than it sounds:

- You cannot decide on an order (who will say which number).

- More than one person must count (not one person on their own counting one to ten).

- If more than one person speaks a number at the same time you have to start again from the beginning (number 1).

You can also use letters of the alphabet instead of numbers. This could also help with remembering the order of the letters in the alphabet.

If you use letters of the alphabet, you should choose a letter to go up to (e.g. **a** to **h** or **i**) and include more letters each time you play.

I first played this game with Theatr Fforwm Cymru.

If you are thinking about giving up on something because it is hard, try to think of a time when you stuck at something and ended up with a good result.

This doesn't have to be something at school – some of my favourite cakes to bake were disasters the first time I made them!

So let not giving up be your thing, in learning and in life!

CHAPTER 9

For Parents and Guardians

If you are under 18 and reading this – stop right now!

There is nothing secret or bad in this chapter, but I think you will find it so boring that it might send you to sleep for a hundred years.

So, I beg you, please skip to the next chapter.

Then, when you have finished this book, give it to Mum or Dad or whoever takes care of you (usually the person who gives you food), and then ask them to read this chapter.

Don't panic

If you have just found out that your child is dyslexic, or you think they might be, this does not mean the end of the world.

There are dyslexic scientists, politicians, writers, inventors and entrepreneurs amongst many other professions.

You will find dyslexic people in all walks of life.

Your child's brain works differently to those of non-dyslexics, but this should never hold them back or prevent them from fulfilling their aspirations and dreams.

In terms of diagnosis and assessment, there are two different aspects to consider. These are internal school tests, and tests carried out by educational psychologists (assessing for an Individual Education Plan usually known as an IEP).

School

Your child's school may do an internal assessment which would normally identify those at risk of dyslexia or with dyslexic tendencies.

Schools use different tests. I am aware of at least three different tests at schools within the same county.

If your child's dyslexia is severe, or they have additional learning requirements, the school may recommend, or refer you to, an educational psychologist for a full assessment.

Schools are able to provide a level of support without a report (IEP) written by an educational psychologist.

Support for dyslexic learners may include:

- Extra time in exams

- Coloured overlays (reading rulers)

- A reader in exams

- Read&Write Gold software

- C-Pen Reader (especially the exam reader pen)

- A learning support assistant in the classroom.

When extra time in exams is required, an application is usually made by the school to the examining board to allow more time for the learner.

The application may take time, so the sooner this is identified and requested, the better.

Coloured overlays (reading rulers) are available from Crossbow Education (see Resources) and can assist reading in dyslexic learners, especially for those with the associated condition Irlen Syndrome.

A reader in exams is usually a member of the learning support team who can read exam questions out loud to the learner.

Read&Write Gold is software aimed at assisting dyslexic learners.

Key features include a toolbar allowing the learner to play text aloud through headphones, links to various dictionaries and an ability to save web addresses for research purposes (see Resources).

A C-Pen Reader can be used to scan text from any source, and can read text aloud using headphones.

As the C-Pen has an attached camera, as opposed to a laser, it can read almost any text.

I really put it to the test using it on photocopies, with underlined and highlighted paragraphs (that was a fun day!).

It also has a dictionary function. When you scan a word, the definition appears underneath on the LED screen (see Resources).

For schools in particular, the Exam Reader pen can be very useful. It has the same operational function as the C-Pen Reader described above, but has been approved by exam boards.

This means it could be used by a young person even if they have not been diagnosed with dyslexia, and the school doesn't need to apply for access arrangements for an individual to use it.

Alongside other examinations, it can be used for the GCSE English comprehension paper.

And finally, learning support assistant in the classroom is an individual who can work with the learner, clarifying anything that hasn't been understood and advising and supporting where required, based upon the individual learner's requirements.

All of the support listed above, except extra time in exams, is subject to the school your child attends having enough funding and resources to deliver any of these provisions.

Individual Education Plans

It is a long time – over twenty years – since my own assessment was carried out by an educational psychologist.

For this book, I wanted more up-to-date information, so I spoke with the principal of the Helen Arkell Centre (see Resources) which, amongst other things, provides Individual Education Plan (IEPs) where required.

The first point to make is that an IEP comes with a financial cost and, in isolation, may not be an effective solution.

Your local education authority may decide that any assistances highlighted in the report are recommendations and therefore do not have to be implemented.

Currently in the UK, dyslexia is the learning difference least likely to receive access to support, despite IEPs which, sadly offer no guarantee that support will be provided.

As with the section on schools, much of the support available will be dependent upon resources and funding.

From my own assessment, I was lucky enough to be provided with all the technology, tools and support suggested in the report.

The only part I found challenging was being given a reading age.

At the age of 19, and whilst undertaking a degree, I was given a reading age of nine.

This was very disheartening. It knocked my confidence and I was all too aware that I would still be expected to read information at degree level.

This also seemed to me to be quite subjective. I have personally known readers of all ages to vary greatly in their abilities, so an age is not perhaps the most accurate way of expressing this data.

Whilst a reading age is currently still used in reports, there is a move towards the use of a standard score more closely akin to how IQ is measured.

So, to return to the question about whether an individual is dyslexic, a parent who is dyslexic would now be seen as presenting a key 'at risk' factor.

Dyslexia can range from mild to severe and so may be picked up at different stages and may also require different strategies.

In my own opinion, if a child finds reading and spelling challenging, typically writes some or all letters back to front and in the wrong order, and finds traditional teaching methods ineffective, and yet the child is creative and appears bright and capable at things which don't involve reading and writing, it is worth asking whether dyslexia might be a possible explanation.

So what can you do?

If you think your child is dyslexic, as a parent or guardian you could liaise with the school. Ask about challenges that you could work on together at home.

Play word games together on a regular basis and explain any new words used.

Encourage reading for fun at home and read together whenever possible.

Possible complications:

- you are also dyslexic

- you work long hours.

If either or both of these are the case then you could consider:

- Purchasing pre-made games (see Resources).

- Adult literacy classes (many community education centres/ colleges offer classes for free).

- Work at a level you are confident with.

- Get support from other family members and friends.

- You may have a family member or friend who really enjoys word games, and is just waiting for an invitation to play them with you and your child.

- You can also find some interesting word games online.

- Purchase a C-Pen Reader (described in the school section of this chapter), as this can be used to scan text or read it aloud, and also has a dictionary function; it can be very useful to use at home as well as in school. This excellent bit of kit can allow for independent learning and study.

It also comes with free upgrades which can be found online (see Resources).

- If your child hasn't already done it, ask them the questions from Chapter 1 to find out how they learn best, and then look at the relevant chapter (e.g. learning through movement in Chapters 2 and 4) for more ideas.

I asked some of the parents of dyslexic children with whom I work to read this chapter and let me know what they thought.

The following comments and suggestions were made:

I love the resources. I think it is important that parents persist even if school is telling them that there is no issue. I was told by the Head of the school that my son was not dyslexic, he was just a low achiever. Some years later he was identified as being dyslexic.

Dyslexic parent, of a dyslexic child

A specialist support department for those with learning differences would be really useful in junior (under age 11) schools.

Dyslexic parent, of a dyslexic child

CHAPTER 10

A Different Letter

Hannah wrote the letter in Chapter 1, asking for my help.

I asked her to write to me again and tell me what had changed and what was different for her now.

This is what she wrote:

Dear Alais,

Thank you for the dyslexic tutoring; it was fun and great support.

I really needed a mental and emotional boost, which this has given me.

In school I personally think I'm a lot more confident in literacy, grammar and punctuation.

I have gained A and B grades, in recent work – WOOOHOOO!

I have created a healthy and happy community around me, with great friends who understand my situation and support me.

I often look back on the amazing things you have taught me.

I have also created new ways to learn too!

- I am now one of the few people that are in 'Top set group'!

- We all know dyslexia can be a blessing... well sometimes ☺

- Thank you – H

This letter moves me to tears every time I read it.

I am so very proud of Hannah and the work she has put in and her open-mindedness about trying new ways of learning.

We are always learning and I would like to share with you what I have learnt so far.

We have different brains and learn best in different ways – this is definitely okay.

Life would be very boring if we were all the same.

Learn things in a way that works for you

I went back to swimming as an adult.

When I started to swim again, I found that I was putting in lots of effort but just splashing and not really moving forward.

I was often tired and grumpy as a result.

I was working so hard but not really getting anywhere.

My friend, who is an excellent swimmer, gave me some good advice: 'Don't fight the water.'

I didn't understand at first, but then I realised that if I stopped fighting against the water and let the flow help me, things would be easier.

You can use this advice for any kind of learning.

So, if you are putting in lots of hard work, but don't feel like you are getting results, be ready to change how you are doing things.

Your time and energy are special, so try to use them in ways that gain results instead of using them to fight against a way of doing things which doesn't work for you.

I am still swimming and try to get better every time but I am also trying to 'Stop fighting against the water' in other things too.

Make learning fun

I have also learnt that it is important to make learning fun.

As humans, we remember things that are enjoyable, so the more fun you can have while learning, the more you will learn and remember.

Let not giving up be your thing

If something comes easily to you, it may not mean as much as something you have had to wait for.

It is the same with learning. You will enjoy things that you are great at the first time you try them, but you might then get bored because it is 'too easy'.

Something that takes hard work and determination will be special when you reach your goal, because you worked for it.

So don't walk away from things which are hard at first – stick at them and find a way of doing them that works for you.

Celebrate success

Success means different things to different people.

It might mean getting a job that you want or getting good grades in exams or doing well in sport, winning competitions, and so on.

But success can also be found in 'smaller' things.

These might include making a cake, learning to ride a bike, reading a chapter in a book or learning how to spell a word.

Enjoy and feel good about success, no matter what it is.

Do something that makes you happy when you have succeeded at something.

This could be going Go-Karting with your friends, as a reward for learning all your times tables (a young person I work with did this).

Or it could be just drawing a smiley face when you have learnt some words for a spelling test.

Thank you

Finally, I would to say a big thank you to you for reading this book.

I hope it has given you some ideas.

I also hope that it has shown you that it is okay to think and learn in the way you do.

You are already a star: you just have to remember to shine!

Resources

Helpful websites

www.bdadyslexia.org.uk – British Dyslexia Association

www.helenarkell.org.uk – Helen Arkell: Provides assessments and advice for dyslexics

www.dyslexia-london.com – Dyslexia Assessments London: An educational psychologist providing assessments for young people and adults

https://feltmagnet.com/drawing/How-to-Improve-Handwriting – 'Practice Exercises for Adults, Teens and Older Kids to Improve Handwriting'

www.cursivewriting.org – Cursive Writing: Handwriting worksheets www.spellzone.com – Spellzone: Useful for word pattern lists (e.g. words ending 'cian')

www.wordhippo.com – WordHippo spelling resources: Useful for word pattern lists

www.guruparents.com – Free online printable times tables cards

Stuff to buy

www.smythstoys.com – Scrabble board game

www.amazon.co.uk
– Lexicon card game (contains letter cards)
– 'My First UK Money Snap' and 'My First Making Words Snap' (contains letter cards)

www.theworks.co.uk – Wooden times tables board

www.tesco.com or www.amazon.co.uk – Cluedo board game

www.argos.co.uk or www.amazon.co.uk – Metronome

www.hobbycraft.co.uk – Craft sticks

www.cpen.com – C-Pen

www.stabilo.com – Stabilo 'Easy Start' refillable handwriting rollerball pen www.crossboweducation.com – Reading Rulers (variety of colours) and educational games (e.g. word puzzles)

www.texthelp.com – Read&Write Gold software

Books

Gardener, H. (2006) *Multiple Intelligences*. New York: Basic Books.

Parkinson, J. (2007) *I Before E (Except after C)*. London: Michael O'Mara Books Ltd.

Morrison, K. (2015) *Flip Flap Fun Times Tables*. Berkhamsted: Make Believe Ideas Ltd.

Finlay, M. (2015) *Everyday English for Grown-Ups*. London: Michael O'Mara Books Ltd.

Winton, A. (2015) *The Self-Help Guide for Teens with Dyslexia*. London: Jessica Kingsley Publishers.

Index